AMERICAN
JUSTICE II

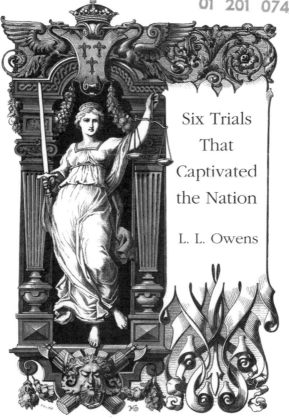

Six Trials
That
Captivated
the Nation

L. L. Owens

Perfection Learning®

Cover design and inside layout: Michelle Glass

About the Author

Lisa L. Owens grew up in the Midwest. She studied English and journalism at the University of Iowa. She works as an editor and freelance writer and lives near Seattle with her husband, Timothy Johnson.

Other books by Ms. Owens include *American Justice: Seven Famous Trials of the 20th Century, America's Civil War,* and *Bigfoot: The Legend Lives On.*

Note

This book contains information about well-known trials and notorious crimes. Please be aware that as a result, many serious and upsetting criminal actions are discussed.

Cover images: ©CORBIS, Photodisc.com (background)

Image Credits: ©Bettmann/CORBIS p. 18 (top); ©AFP/CORBIS p. 40; ©AFP/CORBIS p. 48; ©AFP/CORBIS p. 49; Associated Press pp. 6 (top), 18 (bottom), 21, 26, 28, 29, 30, 36, 39, 44, 45

Art Today (all other images copyright www.arttoday.com)

TABLE OF CONTENTS

INTRODUCTION

During the 20th century, countless trials took place in courtrooms across America. Some were more famous than others. Still others were so intriguing—or disturbing—that the public cried out for more information about them.

This book takes a look at the following real-life crimes and trials.

- the clash between deeply held religious beliefs and scientific theories
- the downfall of a respected government official
- a murder mystery that has spanned five decades
- the abduction—and brainwashing—of a beautiful young heiress
- an act of police brutality that led to three days of uncontrollable riots in the streets of Los Angeles
- a devastating act of terrorism

All of these cases left lasting impressions on the American public. Read on to find out why!

THE SCOPES "MONKEY" TRIAL

Case at a glance

Year: 1925
Trial Location: Dayton, Tennessee
Defendant: John Thomas Scopes
Criminal Charge: Teaching evolution
Verdict: Guilty (The decision was **reversed** on a **technicality** one year later.)
Sentence: $100 fine

Setting the Scene: 1925

In 1925, a great tug-of-war was taking place in America. The struggle was between people with scientific views and people with more traditional views.

These viewpoints were often the direct opposites of each other. And debates were heated.

An issue often debated was the belief in divine creation versus the **theory** of evolution. Both sides had knowledgeable and devoted supporters.

Many people held strong opinions about divine creation. They felt that it should be taught in schools. Others felt that Charles Darwin's theory of evolution should be taught instead.

The Butler Act and John T. Scopes

In February 1925, the Butler Act became law in Tennessee. This act made it unlawful for a teacher in a state-funded school "to teach any theory that denies the story of the divine creation of man as taught in the Bible, and to teach instead that man has descended from a lower order of animals."

This meant that teaching evolution was against the law in Tennessee.

At the time, John T. Scopes was a 24-year-old teacher in Dayton, Tennessee. He believed in Darwin's theory. So he decided to challenge the law.

The American Civil Liberties Union (ACLU) promised to defend Scopes. So on April 24, Scopes taught his high school science students a lesson. The topic was evolution.

Scopes was arrested two weeks later.

The Two Sides

Charles Darwin and the Theory of Evolution

Charles Darwin (1809–1882) was a **naturalist**. He and fellow scientist Alfred Russell Wallace proposed the theory of evolution. Their work was influenced by other theorists of the day. Darwin's name, however, is more closely connected with evolution than any other.

Alfred Russell Wallace

Darwin's 1859 book, *The Origin of Species*, explored evolution fully. The theory is often described as "the survival of the fittest."

Darwin said that, on average, nature's population is constant. Parents (of all species) tend to produce more offspring than is needed to replace them.

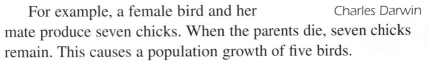

Charles Darwin

For example, a female bird and her mate produce seven chicks. When the parents die, seven chicks remain. This causes a population growth of five birds.

The increase in offspring results in competition. Then members of a species need to compete for survival. Those who survive have the strongest, or *dominant*, traits. And those traits are passed from generation to generation.

This competitive selection of traits can cause species to change, or *evolve*, with time. And with enough time, a species can change into what should be **classified** as a new species.

This part of the theory was used to suggest that the human species may have developed from the same **ancestral** species as modern apes.

What Is Creationism?

Creationism is the belief in divine creation by God. It is a common religious belief about how the world—and everything in it—came to be.

The biblical book of Genesis describes life's beginnings. According to Genesis, God created the world as we know it. And he did so in seven days.

7

- He created heaven on day one.
- He created the earth and populated it with plants on day two.
- He created the sun and the moon on day three.
- He created sea creatures and birds on day four.
- He created land animals, including humans, on day five. Man was intended "to rule the fish in the sea, the birds of heaven . . . [and] all wild animals on earth."
- He created the "finishing touches" on day six.
- And on the seventh day, he rested.

There is little common ground between the theory of evolution and creationism.

The Pretrial Circus

The case was big. The stakes were high. People on both sides wanted the issue decided—once and for all.

The press swarmed to Dayton. A great number of reporters covered the trial. Back then, journalists **filed** their stories over the telegraph. Dayton had to string new lines.

Pretrial news reports called the trial the "monkey" case. Eager **entrepreneurs** flocked to the scene. They sold every type of monkey souvenir imaginable.

Well-known attorney Clarence Darrow led the ACLU **defense** team. The other defense attorneys were Arthur Garfield Hays and Dudley Field Malone.

A. T. Stewart

Popular legal and political figure William Jennings Bryan served as chief **prosecutor** with A. T. Stewart.

Bryan said that the case would be "a duel to the death." He said, "If evolution wins in Dayton, Christianity goes."

Two legal giants were set to square off in court.

For the Defense: Clarence Darrow

Clarence Darrow (1857–1938) was one of the 20th century's brightest lawyers. He was also one of the most famous.

Darrow's other well-known **defendants** included

- William "Big Bill" Haywood (1907), a labor radical charged with murder
- James McNamara and John McNamara (1911), labor leaders charged with bombing
- Nathan Leopold and Richard Loeb (1924), college students charged with murder
- Thomas Massie (1932), charged with kidnapping and murder

Caricature of Clarence Darrow

For the Prosecution: William Jennings Bryan

William Jennings Bryan (1860–1925) was a politician and a lawyer. He served as a Democratic Congressman in the 1890s.

He ran for president three times. He won the Democratic nomination twice.

Late in his life, Bryan became a religious **fundamentalist**. He supported **prohibition**. And he strongly opposed the teaching of evolution in school.

Bryan was called "The Great Commoner." He wanted to preserve traditional thought and customs. His views made the Scopes trial all the more important to him.

William Jennings Bryan

The Courtroom Drama

The trial began on Friday, July 10, 1925. Nearly 1,000 interested citizens crowded the courtroom.

Darrow argued that the Butler Act **violated** the U.S.

Constitution. He said it took away people's First Amendment and Fourteenth Amendment rights. Those rights included freedom of religion and the right to due process of law.

Stewart gave the **prosecution's** opening statement. He said that Scopes had violated the Butler Act. And he had denied the story of creation presented in the Bible.

Defense attorney Malone responded. He said that the prosecution would have to address the two important parts of the Butler Act. It would need to *prove* that Scopes had

- denied the **validity** of creationism
- taught that man had descended from a lower order of mammals

A string of witnesses testified at trial. Here's what happened.

- Scopes' students said they'd been taught that humans evolved from one-cell **organisms**.
- The drugstore owner from whom Scopes had bought his textbook testified. He said that the textbook had been approved for sale by the state.
- A Johns Hopkins University doctor explained the scientific meaning of evolutionary theory.
- In a surprising move, Darrow called Bryan to the stand. Darrow wanted to question him as an expert on the Bible. Bryan accepted. Through clever questioning, Darrow got Bryan to **contradict** himself—and the Bible—under oath. Bryan was humiliated.

Here is the **abridged** testimony of one of Scopes' students. The student's name was Howard Morgan. He was under direct examination by Stewart.

Stewart: Your name is Howard Morgan?

Morgan: Yes, sir.

Stewart:	You are Mr. Luke Morgan's son?
Morgan:	Yes, sir.
Stewart:	Your father is in the bank here? Dayton Bank and Trust Company?
Morgan:	Yes, sir.
Stewart:	How old are you?
Morgan:	14 years.
Stewart:	Did you attend Central High School here in Dayton last year?
Morgan:	Yes, sir.
Stewart:	Did you study this book, *General Science*, under Professor Scopes?
Morgan:	Yes, sir.
Stewart:	Were you studying that book in April of this year, Howard?
Morgan:	Yes, sir.
Stewart:	Did Professor Scopes teach it to you?
Morgan:	Yes, sir.
Stewart:	Now, you say you were studying this book in April. How did Professor Scopes teach that book to you? I mean by that did he ask you questions and you answered them? Or did he give you lectures? Or both? Just explain to the jury how he taught the book to you.
Morgan:	Well, sometimes he would ask us questions, and then he would lecture to us on different subjects in the book.
Stewart:	Did he ever undertake to teach you anything about evolution?
Morgan:	Yes, sir.
Stewart:	Just state in your own words, Howard, what he taught you and when it was.
Morgan:	It was along about the second of April.
Stewart:	Of this year?

Morgan: Yes, sir. Of this year. He said that the earth was once a hot molten mass—too hot for plant or animal life to exist upon it. In the sea, the earth cooled off. There was a little germ of one cell. An organism formed. And this organism kept evolving until it got to be a pretty good-sized animal. Then it came on to be a land animal. It kept on evolving, and from this was man.

Stewart: I ask you further, Howard, how did he classify man with reference to other animals?

Morgan: Well, the book and he both classified man along with cats and dogs, cows, horses, monkeys, lions, horses, and all that.

Stewart: What did he say they were?

Morgan: Mammals.

Stewart: Classified them along with dogs, cats, horses, monkeys, and cows?

Morgan: Yes, sir.

The following is Clarence Darrow's **cross-examination** of Howard Morgan.

Darrow: Let's see, your name is what?

Morgan: Howard Morgan.

Darrow: Now, Howard, what do you mean by "classify"?

Morgan: Well, it means classify these animals we mentioned, that men were just the same as them, in other words.

Darrow: [Professor Scopes] didn't say a cat was the same as a man?

Morgan: No, sir. He said man had a reasoning power, that these animals did not.

Darrow: There is some doubt about that. But that is what he said, is it?

(Laughter in the courtroom.)

Court: Order . . .

Darrow: Now, Howard, he said they were all mammals, didn't he?

Morgan: Yes, sir.

Darrow:	Did he tell you what a mammal was? Or don't you remember?
Morgan:	Well, he just said these animals were mammals and man was a mammal.
Darrow:	No; but did he tell you what distinguished mammals from other animals?
Morgan:	I don't remember.
Darrow:	If he did, you have forgotten it?
Morgan:	I don't remember about that.
Darrow:	You don't remember?
Morgan:	No.
Darrow:	Do you remember what he said that made any animal a mammal, what it was, or don't you remember?
Morgan:	I don't remember.
Darrow:	But he said that all of them were mammals?
Morgan:	All what?
Darrow:	Dogs and horses, monkeys, cows, man, whales. I cannot state all of them. But he said all of those were mammals?
Morgan:	Yes, sir. But I don't know about the whales. He said all those other ones.

(Laughter in the courtroom.)

Court:	Order . . .
Darrow:	Well, did he tell you anything else that was wicked?
Morgan:	No. Not that I remember.
Darrow:	Now, he said the earth was once a molten mass of liquid, didn't he?
Morgan:	Yes.
Darrow:	By molten, you understand melted?
Morgan:	Yes, sir.

13

Darrow:	After that, it got cooled enough, and the soil came and plants grew. Is that right?
Morgan:	Yes, sir, yes, sir.
Darrow:	And that the first life was in the sea. And that it developed into life on the land?
Morgan:	Yes, sir.
Darrow:	And finally into the highest organism which is known to man?
Morgan:	Yes, sir.
Darrow:	Now, that is about what he taught you? It has not hurt you any, has it?
Morgan:	No, sir.
Darrow:	That's all.

At the end of the trial, Darrow asked the jury to return a guilty verdict. This was another surprise.

Darrow knew what he was doing, though. He knew that the case could be **appealed** to the Tennessee Supreme Court.

The judge allowed Darrow's request. So there was no need for the prosecution to continue.

As a result, Bryan was denied his chance to deliver his closing speech. Darrow took pleasure in depriving his rival of the spotlight.

The jury returned a guilty verdict within minutes.

The Sentencing

After the verdict, Judge John T. Raulston **sentenced** Scopes. He ordered Scopes to pay a fine of $100.

The following is an excerpt from the sentencing **transcript**.

Court:	Mr. Scopes, the jury has found you guilty . . . charging you with having taught in the schools of Rhea County, in violation of what is commonly known as the anti-evolution **statute**. [This] makes it unlawful for any

teacher to teach in any of the public schools of the state . . . any theory that denies the story of the divine creation of man. [It is unlawful to] teach instead thereof that man has descended from a lower order of animals. The jury has found you guilty. The statute makes this an offense punishable by fine of not less than $100 nor more than $500. The court now fixes your fine at $100.

Oh—Have you anything to say, Mr. Scopes, as to why the court should not impose punishment upon you?

Scopes: Your honor, I feel that I have been convicted of violating an unjust statute. I will continue in the future, as I have in the past, to oppose this law in any way I can. Any other action would be in violation of my ideal of academic freedom—that is, to teach the truth as guaranteed in our Constitution of personal and religious freedom. I think the fine is unjust.

Bryan's Sudden Death

One evening shortly after the trial ended, William Jennings Bryan finished his dinner. He didn't feel well. So he decided to take a nap.

Bryan died in his sleep.

Reporters tracked down Clarence Darrow. He was hiking in the Smoky Mountains.

A reporter said that perhaps Bryan had died of a broken heart.

Darrow replied, "Broken heart nothing. He died of a busted belly." He quickly added, for the rest of the group, "His death is a great loss to the American people."

Case Closed?

The Tennessee Supreme Court reversed the Scopes decision one year later. The reversal was based on a technicality.

The judge in the Scopes case had set the fine. According to the Supreme Court, the jury should have done it instead.

The Supreme Court decided against sending the case back to the lower court. The court said, "Nothing is to be gained by prolonging the life of this bizarre case."

In the end, the Scopes case was largely considered a victory for evolutionists. It had exposed the issue to the nation and made the public think about this theory.

Noted writer H. L. Mencken covered the trial. He wrote the following.

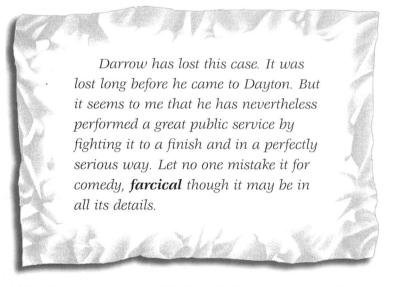

*Darrow has lost this case. It was lost long before he came to Dayton. But it seems to me that he has nevertheless performed a great public service by fighting it to a finish and in a perfectly serious way. Let no one mistake it for comedy, **farcical** though it may be in all its details.*

A similar case appeared before the Supreme Court in 1968—43 years after the Scopes trial. The Supreme Court ruled that an Arkansas law, which was much like the Butler Act, was unconstitutional.

The law, said the court, violated the First Amendment requirement of separation between church and state.

The Scopes "monkey" case is history. But the debate over its central issue continues.

Chapter

ALGER HISS:
SoViEt SPY or
American Scapegoat?

Case at a glance

Years: 1949 and 1950
Trial Location: New York City, New York
Defendant: Alger Hiss
Criminal Charge: Perjury
Verdict: First trial—jury was deadlocked; second trial—guilty
Sentence: 5 years in prison

Life Before the Scandal

Alger Hiss was born in 1904. He graduated from Johns Hopkins University and Harvard Law School. Then he got a job as a law clerk to Supreme Court Justice Oliver Wendell Holmes.

Harvard Hall

Alger Hiss

From there, Hiss went on to a successful government career. He worked in President Franklin D. Roosevelt's **administration**. Then he worked in the departments of agriculture, justice, and state.

Hiss served as Roosevelt's advisor at the 1945 Yalta Conference. He was also a temporary secretary-general of the United Nations.

Franklin D. Roosevelt

In 1946, he was elected president of the Carnegie Endowment for International Peace.

Hiss had built a remarkable career. He'd become a powerful member of the U.S. government.

But all that changed in 1948. That's when a Soviet spy accused Hiss of **espionage**. The spy's name was Whittaker Chambers. The resulting scandal would become part of U.S. history.

Whittaker Chambers

Whittaker Chambers was born in Philadelphia just after the turn of the 20th century. His given name was Jay Vivian Chambers.

In the 1920s, he changed his first name to Whittaker. That was his mother's maiden name. Chambers would use many different names, or *aliases*, throughout his adult life.

Whittaker Chambers

Chambers worked as a journalist. He was an editor at several publications. They included

- *The New Masses*
- *The Daily Worker*
- *Time*

Chambers joined the **Communist Party** in 1923. He remained a member until 1938. He died in 1961.

Chambers Points to Hiss

In 1948, Chambers confessed to having been a Soviet agent. He said that he'd worked for Russia during the 1930s.

He identified Hiss as a member of the same spy ring. He told the House Committee on Un-American Activities that Hiss knowingly passed secret information to the Soviets.

Chambers claimed that Hiss had given him classified information. He claimed that Hiss had taken the papers from the State Department.

As proof, Chambers handed over some papers. He claimed that they had been typed on Hiss's typewriter.

Chambers claimed to have further evidence against Hiss. He produced what would come to be known as "The Pumpkin Papers." They were microfilms of government papers.

According to Chambers, he'd received them from Hiss. And he'd kept them hidden in a pumpkin on his farm.

Committee Hearings

The House committee held closed-door hearings. They listened to Chambers' testimony. Then they allowed Hiss to testify.

The Committee on Un-American Activities

The Committee on Un-American Activities was formed in the U.S. House of Representatives. It began in 1938.

Its purpose was to investigate federal employees. It focused on employees' loyalty to the U.S. government and its causes. The committee was mostly interested in identifying Communists.

Future president Richard M. Nixon served on the committee. He was dedicated to uncovering anti-American plots. He felt strongly that he had done so during the Alger Hiss investigations.

The committee disbanded in 1975.

Hiss flatly denied all charges. He called them "complete fabrication." And he said that he did not commit espionage.

He also denied even knowing anyone named Whittaker Chambers.

Congressman Richard M. Nixon, however, presented Chambers to Hiss. Hiss finally said that he knew Chambers.

But he claimed that he knew Chambers by a different name. Hiss knew Chambers by the name George Crosley.

Meanwhile, Chambers told his story to the media. Hiss then sued Chambers for **slander**.

Hiss was **indicted** by a New York federal **grand jury**. The grand jury charged him with two counts of perjury. They said Hiss had lied under oath. Allegedly, his lies included denials of

- giving secret government papers to Chambers
- speaking to Chambers after January 1, 1937

Two Trials

The trial began May 31, 1949.

Chambers' less-than-perfect record was exposed. His credibility was put to the test. The defense proved that in the past Chambers had

- been a member of the Communist Party
- stolen books from libraries
- been kicked out of Columbia University
- used seven or more aliases
- committed perjury—*twice*

Hiss's attorneys used many character witnesses. They had all known Hiss through various government situations. All swore that Hiss's honesty and his loyalty to the U.S. were too strong to be questioned.

The prosecutors held firm. They presented the papers and the typewriter as the most important pieces of the puzzle.

They felt that they had proven Chambers had papers he could only have received from Hiss. And many of the papers were typed on Hiss's typewriter.

The defense asked a typewriter engineer to study typed material from the typewriter in question. The engineer then built a new typewriter that produced identical type.

A document expert claimed that no expert could tell the difference between papers typed on the two typewriters. This showed that the papers could have come from a typewriter other than Alger Hiss's.

Something to Consider

In the early 1970s, President Richard Nixon was involved in his own scandal. It was known as Watergate.

Several men working for his re-election committee were arrested. They were breaking into the Watergate building. That's where Democratic National Committee headquarters were. (Nixon was a Republican.)

President Richard Nixon

In 1973, the men were convicted of burglary and espionage.

21

The U.S. Senate held hearings. They wanted to find out whether Nixon or anyone in his administration had been directly involved in the break-ins or later cover-ups.

Surprisingly, Alger Hiss's name came up during the hearings. Former Presidential Counsel John Dean testified. He claimed that Nixon had said, "The typewriters are always the key. . . . We built one in the Hiss case."

Dean's comment brought up an interesting question. Could the prosecution have built a typewriter to use against Hiss during his trial?

At the end of the trial, the jury was unable to reach a decision. In other words, they were *deadlocked*.

A second trial began November 17, 1949.

Expert testimony called Chambers' sanity into question. Psychiatrist Dr. Carl Binger said that Chambers suffered from a *psychopathic personality*. The symptoms included antisocial behavior, **chronic** lying, and "the tendency to make false accusations."

Nevertheless, Hiss was found guilty on both counts of perjury. The jury believed that he had lied about his involvement with Chambers.

Hiss eventually served three years and eight months of a five-year sentence. He served his time at the federal prison in Danbury, Connecticut.

In a letter to his young son Tony, Hiss talked about prison. He told of the strict conditions under which a suspected spy lived.

March 28, 1951

For the next 30 days or so, I will be filling out forms, getting typhoid shots . . . having physical exams and I.Q. tests, and finally being assigned to a job. During that time I may have no visits. After that I am permitted 2 hours of visiting time a

*month. . . . I can receive a total of only 7 letters a
week from my 7 permitted* **correspondents**. *[And]
I may write but 3 a week to all my correspondents
combined . . .*

Source: *The View from Alger's Window: A Son's
Memoir* by Tony Hiss (Knopf, 1999)

Hiss left prison in 1954. Over the next 40 years, he tried to
clear his name.

In 1992, the chairman of Russia's military records spoke
out. He supported Hiss. He said that a vast search of Soviet
records had been done. It had turned up no evidence that Hiss
had ever been involved in a spy ring. In fact, the chairman
called accusations against Hiss "groundless."

Some scholars said, however, that no search would unearth
Soviet **intelligence** files. So Hiss's guilt or innocence could not
be proven by the findings of the search.

In 1996, Soviet cables intercepted by the U.S. during World
War II were released. They pointed again to Hiss's guilt. Hiss
died that year.

No Resolution in Sight

The case is still debated today. Some people think that Hiss
was a traitor. They believe that he deserved his perjury
conviction. Some even think that Hiss should have been
charged with espionage.

Others say that Hiss was framed. Why? Hiss's case broke at
a time of great unease in America. Many people feared Soviet
Russia and Communist influence in the U.S.

Some see Hiss's trial and conviction as prime examples of
Cold War **hysteria**. They say that the Committee on
Un-American Activities—or someone else in the government—
singled him out. They say that Hiss was used as an example in
the following ways.

- To reassure the public that the government was
"catching" Communists
- To prove there was a real Communist threat

The Cold War

The "Cold War" between the U.S. and the Soviet Union was not a real war.

Geographic borders were not defended. Enemy troops did not fight each other. And in the end there was no definite winner or loser.

Instead, the Cold War could be described as the political clashing of two great forces.

The Cold War era began after World War II. It lasted through the 1960s.

The era was marked by tension between the U.S. and the Soviet Union (and their **allies**). Each "side" believed that the other wanted to control the rest of the world.

The Strange Case of

Dr. Samuel Sheppard

Case at a glance

Years: 1954 and 1966
Trial Location: Cleveland, Ohio
Defendant: Samuel Sheppard
Criminal Charge: Murder
Verdict: First trial—guilty; second trial—not guilty
Sentence: First trial—life in prison

Murder in a Quiet Cleveland Suburb

In 1954, Samuel Sheppard and his 30-year-old wife,
Marilyn, lived in Bay Village, Ohio. Sheppard was a doctor. He
was liked and respected in his community. Patients had
nicknamed him "Dr. Sam."

The Sheppards had a seven-year-old son named Sam. (They
called him "Chip.") And they happily awaited the birth of their
second child.

Bay Village was known as a lovely, quiet, and extremely
safe suburb of Cleveland.

Then a savage crime occurred in the Sheppards' lakeshore neighborhood.

During the early hours of July 4, Marilyn was murdered. She was beaten to death in her bed.

Sheppard was home when it happened. He woke up to find a stranger in the house. But it was too late to save his wife.

The Sheppards' home

Sheppard's Story

Marilyn Sheppard

When the police arrived on the scene, they questioned Sheppard. Sheppard told his version of the events leading up to—and those that came after—Marilyn's death.

Sheppard and his wife entertained friends the evening of July 3. They all had a good time.

Sheppard fell asleep watching television. Marilyn woke him when she went to bed.

But Sheppard fell back to sleep. He was still on the couch when Marilyn cried out some hours later.

Sheppard rushed upstairs. He saw a "dark form" with "bushy hair." It stood next to Marilyn's bed.

He fought with the form. Sheppard was knocked out by a blow to his neck.

When he came to, Sheppard checked Marilyn's pulse. He couldn't find one. Marilyn was covered with blood.

He ran to Chip's room. Thankfully, the boy was asleep—and safe.

Sheppard heard a noise from the main floor. He hurried downstairs. The "form" ran out the back door.

He chased the form to the lakeside beach. Sheppard said, "I lunged or jumped and grasped him . . . from the back."

The two struggled. Sheppard was knocked out a second time.

When he came to, the bottom half of his body was in the water of Lake Erie. The top half was clinging to the beach.

He ran back home. He checked Marilyn's pulse again. Now, he knew, his wife was gone.

Sheppard called neighbors Spencer and Esther Houk. Quickly, they arrived at the Sheppard home. They talked with Sheppard. And they saw the blood-spattered room where Marilyn lay dead. Then they notified the police.

While the police searched the house, Sheppard's two brothers picked him up. The brothers were also doctors. The three of them went to their family-owned hospital. Sheppard was treated for injuries to his face and spinal cord.

The Press Makes Up Its Mind

News of the crime filled Ohio newspapers. People were frightened. They couldn't believe such a thing could happen in Bay Village.

The headlines painted a sympathetic picture of Dr. Sam. Here are a few of them from the Cleveland *Press*, the Cleveland *Plain Dealer*, and the Cleveland *News*.

- Doctor's Wife Murdered in Bay; Drug Thieves Suspected in Bludgeoning
- Bay Doctor's Wife Is Murdered; Beaten, He Tells of Fight with Intruder
- Find Tooth Chips Under Body of Bay Doctor's Slain Wife; Grappled with Brutal Slayer, Physician Says
- They Shared Duties, Pleasures of Life
- Sheppards Face Tragedy Bravely

At first, people decided that the slaying was a freak happening. It was probably done by a wandering psychopath. It was definitely a stranger. Someone had intended to rob the Sheppard home but then got carried away.

Sheppard's frequent media interviews helped further those beliefs. He expressed his deep sorrow at the loss of his life partner and his child's mother.

Susan Hayes

He shared his utter amazement that someone could have come to Bay Village and committed this crime. He also offered a $10,000 reward to anyone who helped catch the killer.

Soon, though, Samuel Sheppard was a suspect. His story varied little during the many times he'd told it. But to police it seemed unbelievable.

Then a woman named Susan Hayes came forward. She claimed to be Sheppard's secret girlfriend. She also claimed that Sheppard had talked of divorcing Marilyn.

Public opinion changed as quickly as the news coverage. Headlines read differently now.

- What Is Happening to Our Sense of Justice?
- Doctor Lies, Susan Charges; Tells of Gifts, Marriage Talk
- Somebody Is Getting Away with Murder

It was no surprise when the police arrested Sheppard and charged him with murder.

Sheppard Stands Trial—Twice

Sheppard's murder trial began on October 18, 1954. The press crowded the courtroom. So did **hordes** of curious onlookers.

The prosecution had no murder weapon. In fact, it had no real evidence connecting Sheppard with the crime. Prosecutor John Mahon offered Sheppard's relationship with Susan Hayes as a **motive**. Then he pointed out holes in Sheppard's story.

Mahon raised many questions. These are a few.

- Why was there no sign of a break-in at the house?
- How could Sheppard have slept through the vicious attack on his wife?
- Where was the T-shirt Sheppard wore while entertaining guests the evening before the killing?
- If Sheppard had been passed out on the beach, why were no traces of sand found in his hair?

The county coroner claimed to know what had made a bloody imprint found on Marilyn's pillow. He testified that it was formed by a two-bladed surgical instrument. It was assumed that Sheppard would be able to get this.

From the beginning, Judge Edward Blythin thought Sheppard was guilty. He even went so far as to say so to a reporter—**off the record**. He made sure that he gave no favors to the defense.

When the jury pronounced Sheppard guilty of second-degree

Coroner with Marilyn's pillow

murder, Judge Blythin quickly sentenced the doctor. He sentenced him to life imprisonment in the Ohio Penitentiary.

Judge Blythin's actions had helped seal Sheppard's fate. But his careless comments to the reporter about Sheppard's guilt would eventually set Sheppard free.

Attorney F. Lee Bailey heard about the judge's comments. He tried to prove that Sheppard had received an unfair trial.

Attorney F. Lee Bailey and Sheppard

The Supreme Court agreed with Bailey. Sheppard's conviction was overturned. The court called it "prejudicial."

So, in 1966, Sheppard stood trial again.

Bailey was far better prepared than Sheppard's first team of defense attorneys.

The prosecution presented basically the same case it had years earlier. The lawyers were not prepared to deal with F. Lee Bailey.

Bailey skillfully raised doubts about each point in the prosecution's case. He even presented other ideas about murder suspects. His arguments were so powerful that the jury took note.

The jury **deliberated** for just 12 hours. They found Sheppard not guilty. And Sheppard was set free.

But his freedom was short-lived. Sheppard died just four years later. He was 46 years old. The cause of death was liver failure.

The Case Lives On

Public interest in the case remained high in the decades following the murder trials. Many books and in-depth articles were written. Even a popular 1960s TV series and a hit 1993 movie were made. A remake of the TV series premiered in fall 2000. All were called *The Fugitive*. They were very loosely based on the Sheppard story.

Sheppard's son, Chip (known in his adult life as Samuel Reese Sheppard), fought hard. He tried to solve his mother's murder. And he tried to completely clear his father's name.

In 1995, Samuel filed a wrongful imprisonment suit against the state of Ohio. He sought $2 million in **damages**. He lost the case April 12, 2000.

As of that day, Marilyn Sheppard's murder was still unsolved. And there were no new leads in sight.

A Timeline of the Sheppard Mystery

This fascinating history of the Sheppard case illustrates why interest in the story and its characters has endured. Startling new developments popped up in the 1950s, 1960s, 1970s, 1980s, 1990s . . .

It seems that the trend may continue well into the 21st century!

July 4, 1954:	Marilyn Reese Sheppard is slain.
July 30, 1954:	Dr. Samuel Sheppard is arrested and charged with murder.
December 21, 1954:	Samuel Sheppard is found guilty.
November 8, 1959:	Richard Eberling, a known thief and the Sheppards' former window washer, is caught with two of Marilyn Sheppard's rings.
June 6, 1966:	The U.S. Supreme Court grants Samuel Sheppard a second trial.

November 16, 1966:	Samuel Sheppard is acquitted.
April 6, 1970:	Samuel Sheppard dies of liver failure. He spent the last years of his life working as a doctor, then as a pro wrestler.
July 7, 1984:	Richard Eberling is convicted of murdering Ethel Durkin.
October 19, 1995:	Sam Reese Sheppard files a wrongful imprisonment lawsuit to clear his father's name.
February 4, 1997:	**DNA** tests show the possibility that blood from Sheppard's home could be Richard Eberling's.
September 17, 1997:	Samuel Sheppard is **exhumed**.
March 5, 1998:	DNA tests show that Samuel Sheppard's blood was not present in bloodstains around the Sheppard home.
July 25, 1998:	Richard Eberling dies in prison.
October 5, 1999:	Marilyn Sheppard is exhumed. DNA and other tests are said to point to Samuel Sheppard as Marilyn's killer.
February 14, 2000:	The wrongful imprisonment trial begins.
April 12, 2000:	The trial ends. The claim that Samuel Sheppard was innocent is rejected.

Patricia Hearst:
THE KIDNAPPING
ORDEAL *of a Young Heiress*

/ Case at a glance \

Year: 1976
Trial Location: San Francisco, California
Defendant: Patricia C. Hearst
Criminal Charges: Bank robbery, felonious use of a firearm
Verdict: Guilty
Sentence: 7 years in prison

February 4, 1974: The Ordeal Begins

Patricia Hearst was a smart, beautiful 19-year-old. She was a sophomore at the University of California at Berkeley. She was engaged to be married. And she was an heiress to the William Randolph Hearst newspaper empire.

Patty's life took a strange and awful turn one February night in 1974. She was spending the evening at her apartment.

A young woman tapped on the sliding-glass door. Patty's fiancé, Steven Weed, opened the door.

The woman said, "May I use your telephone? There's been an accident."

Weed believed for a moment that she needed help. Then the woman and two male members of the Symbionese Liberation Army (SLA) forced their way inside.

They were heavily armed. They beat and tied up Weed.

A neighbor, Steven K. Suenega, heard the noise and tried to help. He was beaten too.

The SLA left the apartment. And they took Patty with them. Patty kicked and screamed and fought the whole way.

The kidnappers threw Patty into the trunk of a 1963 Chevrolet Impala. Then the two cars used by the SLA that night sped away. The SLA shot at the apartment house as they drove off.

The SLA was known as a radical urban terrorist group. They had coined the word *Symbionese*. It was based on the biology term *symbiosis*. That means "the partnership of unlike groups for their mutual benefit." This was appropriate. Members of the group came from all different backgrounds. But they had one goal. According to their slogan, that goal was "Death to the **fascist** insect that preys upon the life of people!"

The SLA likely had no more than a dozen members. A February 18, 1974, study pointed to some specialized skills among SLA members.

The study was done by the Committee on Internal Security for the House of Representatives. It said that

- at least two members had had combat training
- at least one member was a skilled machinist
- at least one member had an extensive knowledge of language

The Days Following the Kidnapping

Randolph and Catherine Hearst were Patty's parents. They were terrified at the news of her capture. They worried that their daughter would be further hurt or killed.

The SLA had already been linked with other crimes, including murder. They claimed that kidnapping Patty was "part of its war against the fascist state."

They also called it an act of revenge against the wealthy Hearsts. Yet they made no immediate demands of the family.

On February 7, the SLA sent letters to a local radio station and an underground newspaper. The station also received a credit card stolen from Patty's apartment.

The letter to the station began as follows.

> **Subject:** *Arrest and protective custody; and if necessary execution.*
>
> **Target:** *Patricia Campbell Hearst, daughter of Randolph Hearst, corporate enemy of the people. Warrant issued by the court of the people.*

The letter claimed that Patty was unharmed. It also said

> *Should any attempt be made to rescue the prisoner, or to arrest or harm any SLA element, the prisoner is to be executed. . . .*
> *[Miss Hearst will be] maintained at adequate physical and mental condition [through] protective custody of combat and medical units . . . [Furthermore] all communications from this court must be published in full. In all newspapers. And all other forms of media. Failure to do so will endanger the safety of the prisoner.*

The SLA released a tape of Patty's voice on February 12. By now the country was riveted to the saga unfolding on the news.

The tape helped reassure the Hearsts that Patty was alive. But they were still frightened.

They heard a male voice on the tape. He said that he was willing to kill Patty. He considered it punishment.

What was the punishment for? According to him, it was "for the crimes that her mother and father have by their actions committed against we, the American people and the oppressed people of the world."

Patty Hearst (center) with her parents, Catherine and Randolph Hearst

Who Were the Hearsts?

At the time of Patty's kidnapping, the Hearsts had been prominent on the American scene since the 1800s. The family had a history of involvement in business, media, politics, and **philanthropy**.

Here's a brief look at three generations of influential Hearst men. Their fame and extreme wealth contributed to the media attention and public interest in Patty's ordeal.

Patty's Great-Grandfather: George Hearst (1820–1891)

George started out as a prospector and geologist in California. He invested in gold and silver mines in Nevada, South Dakota, and Montana. His investments paid off.

In 1880, he bought the *San Francisco Examiner*. His son William would later run it. So would his grandson Randolph.

George and his wife, Phoebe, donated a lot of money to educational causes. They gave money to the University of California and American University. And they set up many free libraries.

George ran for governor of California in 1882. He lost the race. But he later became a U.S. senator. He served from 1886 to 1891.

Patty's Grandfather: William Randolph Hearst (1863–1951)

William was an important U.S. publisher. His publishing empire included

- 28 newspapers
- 18 magazines
- movie companies
- news services
- radio stations

William had a huge impact on American journalism. He introduced the practice of using big banner headlines and special illustrations.

These methods helped attract readers' attention. They made the news of the day seem more interesting and exciting. All this helped sell newspapers too.

William was also a New York congressman. He served from 1903 to 1907.

By the 1970s, Randolph Hearst was the head of the Hearst empire.

He was president and editor of the *San Francisco Examiner*. And he was an heir to his family's fortune. He had great clout in the publishing world.

He and his wife, Catherine, have five daughters: Catherine, Patricia, Virginia, Anne, and Victoria.

The SLA's Demands

Soon the SLA released its demands. The members wanted money. But not for themselves.

The group asked the Hearsts to give millions of dollars' worth of food. It was to go to all of California's poor, aged, disabled veterans, and ex-convicts.

This was to be a sign of "good faith." The SLA would not talk about Patty's release until this happened.

Randolph offered to give $2 million to California's needy. Then, he promised, he'd give another $4 million—but only *if* Patty was safely released.

Randolph followed through. Truckloads of food arrived for distribution. People fought one another to get to the food. Riots nearly broke out.

But Patty Hearst was not set free. The SLA failed to keep its promise.

Patty's Life in Captivity

Patty's life as an SLA prisoner was horrifying. To begin with, she was reportedly locked in a closet for weeks.

According to Patty's 1982 book, *Every Secret Thing*, she was tortured, raped, and *brainwashed*. This meant that the SLA forced her to change her thoughts and beliefs.

Two months after Patty's abduction, the nation gasped. They saw new images of her. Photos of Patty had surfaced in the newspapers.

Thankfully, she was alive. But Patty was now called "Tania." And she carried a rifle and wore combat gear. News reports claimed Patty had joined the SLA. She had even helped her **captors** rob a San Francisco bank!

Patty's family and the nation had feared for Patty's safety. Authorities had been searching for her, hoping to rescue her.

Then, out of the blue, Patty showed up at a bank. But she didn't appear to be in distress. She was robbing and threatening people.

In two months, Patricia Hearst seemed to go from innocent kidnapping victim to armed terrorist. The whole situation was bizarre.

On May 17, 1974, the SLA was involved in a Los Angeles house fire and a shootout with police. Six SLA members were killed.

Meanwhile, Patty had disappeared. She and at least two other SLA members had fled. They crossed the country. They went as far east as New York.

On September 18, 1975, Patty was back in San Francisco. The FBI captured her and three other SLA members that day.

Patty was arrested for armed robbery.

The Trial

Patty's trial began on February 4, 1976. This was exactly two years after she was kidnapped.

The Hearsts had hired attorney F. Lee Bailey. Bailey was confident that he could defend Patty.

Bailey presented Patty as a "prisoner of war." He said that she had taken part in SLA's activities for one reason only. She had wanted to stay alive.

Prosecutor James Browning Jr. argued his case. He said that Patty had always known what she was doing. That she had willingly participated in the robbery and other SLA events.

Patty took the stand in her own defense. She testified that her participation in the crimes was the only way she could have survived.

Some expert witnesses backed this up. Others testified to the contrary. They said Patty had enjoyed the fame and excitement that becoming SLA's "Tania" had given her.

Meanwhile, the public didn't understand. How could Patty have been brainwashed? They followed the trial closely, from beginning to end, hoping to find out.

President Jimmy Carter

The press reported damaging evidence against Patty. Public opinion was split.

On March 20, 1976, the jury found Patricia Hearst guilty as charged. She was sentenced to seven years in prison.

Patty was in and out of jail for three years as her case was appealed. She was released for good on February 1, 1979. President Jimmy Carter **commuted** her sentence. He believed that she had suffered greatly. He felt that she never would have committed criminal acts had she not been forced to.

By 2000, Carter had asked both President George Bush and President Bill Clinton to grant Hearst a full **pardon**. Carter said that since her release from prison "[Patty] has been a model citizen in every way."

But U.S. Justice Department prosecutors still said that Patty acted of her own free will.

The Never-Ending Story

In 1999 and into early 2000, interest in Patty Hearst's story was renewed. (For many, it had never died down.) Patty was called as a witness at the trial of former SLA member Kathleen Soliah. Soliah was now known as Sara Jane Olson.

Olson faced trial for an alleged SLA bomb conspiracy dating back to 1975. She had hidden from authorities for 25 years.

Judge James Ideman ruled that no cameras would be present in the courtroom. He felt it would be upsetting for Patty to testify in public again after so many years.

At this writing, the Olson trial is scheduled to begin in January 2001.

Patricia Hearst Shaw Moves On

Shortly after she left prison, Patty married. She wed Bernard Shaw, her former bodyguard. Patty and her husband raised two daughters.

Patty works as an actor and an author. Her acting experience includes roles in several movies, such as *Cry-Baby* and *Serial Mom*. Her books include *Every Secret Thing, Patty Hearst: Her Own Story*, and *Murder at San Simeon*.

At the beginning of the 21st century, Patty said that she enjoyed her life. And she would like nothing more than to leave her kidnapping ordeal in the past.

On being called as a witness in the Sara Jane Olson trial, Patty said, "This is all so old. I don't want to be drawn into all of this."

Chapter **5**

THE LOS ANGELES POLICE OFFICERS'

"RODNEY KING BEATING" TRIALS

Case at a glance

Years: 1992 and 1993
Trial Locations: First trial—Simi Valley, California; second trial—Los Angeles, California
Defendants: Theodore J. Briseno, Stacey C. Koon, Laurence M. Powell, Timothy E. Wind
Criminal Charges: First trial—assault, use of excessive force by a police officer, filing a false report; second trial—violating a citizen's **civil rights**
Verdicts: First trial—not guilty; second trial—Stacey C. Koon and Laurence M. Powell, guilty; Theodore J. Briseno and Timothy E. Wind, not guilty
Sentences: Koon and Powell each sentenced to 30 months in prison

What Happened?

On March 3, 1991, the Los Angeles police chased Rodney King for three miles. They finally caught him. They began arrest procedures.

But something went terribly wrong.

Rodney King was a young African American. Four white police officers brutally beat him. At least a dozen officers watched.

The whole thing was caught on videotape. The officers, of course, had no idea at the time that anyone was recording their actions.

Official arrest reports make these claims.

- King refused to get out of his car.
- King put up a violent struggle against the officers.

The reports explained that the officers had needed to use force to **subdue** King.

The videotape contradicted the arrest reports, though. The tape showed that King was beaten to the ground.

The officers punched King. They kicked him. They swung metal batons at his head. They even used stun guns. King was unable to fight back.

Officers Are Indicted

Faced with the public videotape and the differing police reports, a grand jury looked into the matter. They indicted four of the officers involved.

- Theodore J. Briseno
- Stacey C. Koon
- Laurence M. Powell
- Timothy E. Wind

The men were charged with assault, using excessive force, and filing a false report.

News of these events sold newspapers and kept Americans glued to the television. It seemed that the media showed clips from the beating video with every mention of the story.

People everywhere were shocked by the apparent police brutality. Civil rights leaders charged that the incident was racially motivated. Los Angeles citizens were angered by the actions of the officers who were supposed to protect the city.

There was so much media attention that the trial was moved to Simi Valley, California. The location was somewhat removed from Los Angeles. The hope was that the move would ensure a fair trial.

Rodney King on the right, with his attorney

The Jury Hears Both Sides

At trial, a California Highway Patrol officer testified against Powell. That officer was Melanie Singer. She said that Powell had used unnecessary force against King.

Other information for the prosecution claimed the following.

- Powell and Wind had lost control of their actions.

- Koon, the highest-ranking officer of the group, did not stop his men.

- The officers filed false reports because they knew that their actions had been illegal.

Information for the defense included the following claims.

• The officers believed that King was on drugs and dangerous.

• Koon and Briseno had tried to end Powell's beating of King.

• The officers' actions were the only way to gain control of King.

The jury found the four officers not guilty. It was a surprise verdict. The violent reaction to the decision went down in history.

The Los Angeles Riots

The acquittal angered the public. Riots broke out in Los Angeles immediately.

Angry mobs terrorized the city for three days straight. They set fires. They smashed windows. They looted businesses. They hurt—and killed—other people.

Destruction on a street in Los Angeles as a result of the riots.

On the second day, King pleaded with rioters. He asked them to stop.

"It's just not right," he said. "It's not right. I just want to say, can we all get along? Can we get along?"

Here are some facts about the riots.

• 1,100 buildings were either damaged or destroyed.

• 2,000 people were injured.

• 58 people died.

• $1 billion in property damage was caused.

Reginald Denny was one of the 2,000 people injured. Denny, a white truck driver, drove into the riot area. He was trying to do his job. But rioters refused to let him safely pass through.

Denny was pulled from his truck. Two African American men beat and kicked him. They stomped on him. And they smashed his head with a brick. Denny suffered 90 broken bones in his face.

The violence was caused by people who were angered at police brutality. Denny—like King—was powerless to stop it.

News helicopters hovering above the scene captured it all on videotape.

Trial After Trial . . .

The outcry over the results of the first trial was so great that the issue remained unresolved.

Soon, the government charged Briseno, Koon, Powell, and Wind with violating Rodney King's civil rights.

A second trial began on February 3, 1993.

At the end of the trial, the jury deliberated. Los Angeles—and the world—nervously awaited the verdict. Many feared more rioting if the officers were again found not guilty.

This time, Briseno and Wind were acquitted. Koon and Powell were convicted.

Los Angeles breathed a bit easier. People felt that justice had been better served with this decision.

Another decision would happen in April 1994. That's when a jury awarded King $3.8 million in damages. King had sued the city of Los Angeles. And he'd won.

King was later asked whether "anything good" had come from his ordeal. He replied, "It has shined the light on police brutality."

Several years after the trials, King commented that police attitudes had improved. He also said, "As far as us as individuals, we have a lot of work to do."

SENSELESS DESTRUCTION:

THE OKLAHOMA CITY
BOMBING

Case at a glance

Year: 1995

Trial Location: Denver, Colorado

Defendants: Timothy McVeigh and Terry Lynn Nichols

Criminal Charges: Federal murder, conspiracy, and weapons
   charges

Verdicts: Timothy McVeigh—guilty on all counts;
   Terry Lynn Nichols—guilty of conspiracy and involuntary
   manslaughter

Sentences: Timothy McVeigh—death by lethal injection;
   Terry Lynn Nichols—life in prison without parole and
   repayment to the government of $14 million in damages

Tragedy Strikes Oklahoma City

On April 19, 1995, people in Oklahoma City started their
day. Busy people rushed to work. Kids went to school. It was
business as usual. At least, it was until 9:03 a.m. That's when
everything changed.

Alfred P. Murrah Federal Building after the bombing

A bomb exploded. It was in a rental truck downtown. The truck was parked outside the nine-story Alfred P. Murrah Federal Building. The building was destroyed.

There were 168 deaths. Many of the victims were small children.

Rescue efforts went on for two weeks. Many people worked tirelessly to find survivors. It was a difficult job, often under dangerous conditions.

But rescue teams didn't give up. They saved lives. Some survivors were trapped in the rubble. And their injuries made it impossible for them to move. Sometimes they couldn't even speak.

The senseless destruction angered the entire nation. It seemed that all Americans mourned with the bombing victims' families. It was horrible. "Unfathomable" was often used to describe the situation.

Suspects

Ninety minutes after the explosion, Timothy McVeigh was pulled over. An Oklahoma Highway Patrol officer noticed that McVeigh's car had no license plate.

Two days later, McVeigh was identified as a suspect in the bombing. He was 27 years old.

Soon McVeigh's friend Terry Nichols was also under suspicion. Nichols and McVeigh were good friends. They had been in the army together.

Nichols decided to turn himself in. He surrendered to police in Kansas.

Timothy McVeigh in the center

The Case to Indict

The case against McVeigh and Nichols was strong. Their actions were retraced. There was a lot of evidence. Evidence included phone records, bills, explosives, and other items that linked the two men to each other—and to the crime.

The grand jury concluded that the men "knowingly, intentionally, willfully, and maliciously" worked together and with unknown others to commit this terrible crime.

Here's how McVeigh and Nichols made it happen.

- The men planned an act of violence against persons and property of the United States.
- The men selected the Alfred P. Murrah Federal Building and its occupants as the targets.
- The men asked others to help.
- The men obtained and hid the pieces of a truck bomb.
- The men used stolen property to help finance their crimes.
- The men used false names to conceal their activities.
- The men built an explosive truck bomb.
- Timothy McVeigh placed the bomb outside the Alfred P. Murrah Federal Building in downtown Oklahoma City.
- Timothy McVeigh set off the bomb.

Criminal Charges

McVeigh and Nichols were both charged with the bombing. A federal grand jury in Oklahoma City handed down the indictments. The two men would stand trial on 11 federal charges. They included

- Count 1: Conspiracy to use a weapon of mass destruction
- Count 2: Use of a weapon of mass destruction
- Count 3: Destruction by explosive
- Counts 4–11: First-degree murder (for the deaths of eight federal workers)

Why Did It Happen?

The Oklahoma City bombing is known as the worst terrorist attack on U.S. soil. A May 17, 1995, *New York Times* article said that McVeigh admitted to the bombing. It said that he told two people that he did it. And he told them why he chose the Alfred P. Murrah Federal Building. He chose it because

- it housed numerous government offices
- it was less architecturally stable than other federal buildings

McVeigh and Nichols meant to cause harm. They meant to kill people. They also meant to shock the nation.

Why? Because they felt that the U.S. government deserved to be punished. They did not care that helpless, innocent people—including small children—would die.

Five years after the crime, McVeigh was interviewed for the CBS newsmagazine *60 Minutes*. The interview was taped February 22, 2000.

McVeigh said of the year 1995, "I believe I had anger welling in me."

For one thing, he was angry at trying out for and failing to get into the army's special forces unit.

He was also upset over his role in the Gulf War. He felt that he'd had no right to enter another land and kill enemy soldiers—even as part of war.

McVeigh was further angered by the handling of two federal cases.

- In 1992, a federal agent killed the wife and son of white supremacist Randy Weaver. There had been a standoff in Ruby Ridge, Idaho. A judge dismissed manslaughter charges against the agent. This upset McVeigh. He said, "Federal agents taking the role of judge, jury, and executioner . . . [Then] you have these . . . federal agents not held accountable. They become immune from the law."

- In 1993, there was the "siege at Waco [Texas]." Seventy Branch Davidians, members of a religious sect, died in a fire. There had been a 51-day standoff with federal agents. McVeigh said that he was "shaken, disillusioned, angered that that could happen in this country." He said, "You deprived them of life, liberty, and property. You didn't guarantee [their] rights. You deprived them of them."

Asked during the interview if he would like to do anything differently, he said, "I think anybody in life says, 'I wish I could've gone back and done this differently, done that differently.' There are moments, but not one that stands out."

Crime and Punishment

The public watched McVeigh's and Nichols' trials closely. People hoped that justice would be served.

Both men were convicted of their federal crimes. But they received different sentences.

McVeigh was convicted of murder and conspiracy to commit murder. He was also found guilty of the weapons-related charges against him. His sentence was the death penalty.

An estimated $10 million was spent on Timothy McVeigh's defense.

Nichols was convicted of conspiracy to use a weapon of mass destruction and eight counts of involuntary manslaughter.

The jury could not agree on a sentence for Nichols. So it became U.S. District Judge Richard Matsch's decision. He did not have authority to sentence Nichols to death. He sentenced him to life in prison without the possibility of parole.

Nichols showed no emotion when he heard his sentence. Judge Matsch called Nichols a "proven enemy of the Constitution."

Trials of the Century

Many 20th-century trials were labeled "the trial of the century." Examples include

- The "Scopes" Monkey Trial
- The Samuel Sheppard Trials
- The Los Angeles Police Officers' "Rodney King Beating" Trial

On February 2, 1999, the Today show ran a segment about the 20th century's most famous trials. They had taken a survey to see what viewers thought.

The trials of Timothy McVeigh and Terry Nichols did not show up on the survey. Why do you think that is?

There were 3,857 respondents. Here are the results.

Question: What do you think is the "trial of the century"?

Response:

24%—The 1995 Trial of O. J. Simpson

21%—The 1946 Nazi War Crimes Trial

20%—The 1999 Clinton Impeachment Trial

14%—The 1925 Scopes "Monkey" Trial

7%—The 1935 Lindbergh Baby Kidnapping Trial

4%—The 1970 Trial of Charles Manson

3%—The 1951 Trial of Ethel and Julius Rosenberg

2%—The 1992 and 1993 Los Angeles Police Officers' "Rodney King Beating" Trials

1%—The 1921 Sacco and Vanzetti Trial

1%—The 1924 Trial of Nathan Leopold and Richard Loeb

1%—The 1931–1937 Scottsboro Trials

1%—The 1954 and 1966 Trials of Samuel Sheppard

1%—The 1969 "Chicago Seven" Trial

0%—The 1906 Trial of Harry Thaw

0%—The 1907 Trial of "Big Bill" Haywood

0%—The 1921 Trial of "Fatty" Arbuckle

Source: MSNBC.com

Note: Percentages may not total to 100% due to non-responses.

GLOSSARY

abridged   shortened

administration   official organization

ally   state, country, or person who associates or joins forces with another by mutual agreement

ancestral   relating to or inherited from an earlier generation

appeal   to take legal action in which a case is taken to a higher court to review the lower court's decision

captor   kidnapper

chronic   frequent

civil rights   personal freedom of U.S. citizens guaranteed by the 13th and 14th amendments to the Constitution

classified   arranged in groups sharing common traits

Communist Party   group who believes in a government that controls all business and industry

commute   to reduce a penalty for another one that is less severe

contradict   to state opposing ideas, thoughts, or beliefs

correspondent   someone who writes a letter

cross-examination   questioning of a witness who has already testified in order to check or discredit testimony

damages   monetary settlement decided upon by the court

defendant   person who is standing trial

defense   team that represents a defendant (see glossary entry) at trial; also, the set of arguments presented in favor of the defendant at trial

deliberate   to consider carefully

DNA   abbreviation of "deoxyribonucleic acid"—a person's genetic makeup

entrepreneur   businessperson

espionage   act of spying

exhume   to remove from a grave

farcical   absurd; laughable

fascist   believing in a strong dictatorial government and the use of force to maintain it

file	to send in; to submit
fundamentalist	one who believes that the literal interpretation of the Bible is basic to Christian life and teaching
grand jury	group that examines the accusations against people charged with crimes and decides if the evidence is strong enough to bring these people to trial
horde	large crowd
hysteria	behavior showing uncontrollable fear
indict	to charge with a crime
intelligence	information about an enemy or possible enemy
motive	reason
naturalist	one who believes that scientific laws explain all things
off the record	not for publication
organism	living being
pardon	in the government setting, the official act of forgiving a crime
philanthropy	charity
prohibition	government ban on the making, sale, transportation, and consumption of alcohol
prosecutor	attorney for the prosecution (see glossary entry)
prosecution	team that brings a legal action against a defendant
reverse	to set aside or make void a legal decision
scapegoat	person set up to take the blame
sentence	to punish or pass judgment
slander	the act of defaming another person by making false statements about him or her
statute	law
subdue	to bring under control
technicality	small detail
theory	scientific explanation for a happening
transcript	written record
validity	truth
violate	to disregard

INDEX